For

Lauren

LOVE

Papa &
Gramma
Nov/99

PEACE BE WITH YOU

Compiled by
Claudine Gandolfi

Illustrated by Jenny Faw

Design by Arlene Greco

PETER PAUPER PRESS, INC.
WHITE PLAINS, NEW YORK

INTRODUCTION

When your inner dwelling houses tranquillity, understanding is close at hand. When understanding lights your hallways, peace is the light by which you see.

Here are words to beckon tranquillity, nurture understanding, kindle the light of peace, and illuminate your spirit. May your

thoughts, words, and deeds
be graced by the spirit of
light. Peace is a gift of the
spirit.

Peace is alive inside each of
us. With this book I offer
you the sign of peace.

C. G.

Think for a while on the
meaning of this word
"peace."

T. S. Eliot

Peace is not a passive but an active virtue.

FULTON J. SHEEN

Whenever you bring harmony into any unpeaceful situation, you contribute to the cause of peace.

PEACE PILGRIM

The pursuit of peace is complicated because it has to do with people, and nothing in this universe baffles man as much as man himself.

ATTRIBUTED TO
ADLAI STEVENSON

I do not want the peace
which passeth understand-
ing, I want the understanding which bringeth peace.

HELEN KELLER

God blesses peace and
curses quarrels.

MIGUEL DE CERVANTES

The wolf also shall dwell
with the lamb, and the
leopard shall lie down with
the kid.

Isaiah 11:6

The same stream of life that
runs through my veins night
and day, runs through the
world and dances in
rhythmic measure.

RABINDRANATH TAGORE

God give me the serenity to
accept things which
cannot be changed;
Give me courage to change
things which must be
changed;
And the wisdom to distin-
guish one from the other.

REINHOLD NIEBUHR

The mind is never right but
when it is at peace within
itself.

LUCIUS ANNAEUS SENECA

The peaceful are the strong.

OLIVER WENDELL HOLMES

Peace is such a precious
jewel that I would give
anything for it but truth.

M. HENRY

In quietness and confidence
shall be your strength.

ISAIAH 30:15

Peace is the fairest form of happiness.

WILLIAM ELLERY CHANNING

Peace puts forth buds in the
full fruitfulness of Truth.

HILDEGARD OF BINGEN

This is the way of peace:
Overcome evil with good,
falsehood with truth, and
hatred with love.

PEACE PILGRIM

True and lasting inner peace can never be found in external things. It can only be found within. And then, once we find and nurture it within ourselves, it radiates outward.

ANONYMOUS

Peace is better than a
fortune.

ST. FRANCIS DE SALES

I harmonize with nature
and all others in my world.
I accept greater peace in
my life now.
And so it is.

DIANE DREHER

Peace comes to us through love, understanding of our fellow men, faith. Peace does not include selfishness nor indifference. Peace is never wrapped at a counter for a price. It is earned by giving of ourselves.

ANNETTE VICTORIN

Peace is a daily, a weekly, a monthly process, gradually changing opinions, slowly eroding old barriers, quietly building new structures. And however undramatic the pursuit of peace, that pursuit must go on.

JOHN FITZGERALD KENNEDY

Look within. Within is the
fountain of good, and it will
ever bubble up, if thou wilt
ever dig.

MARCUS AURELIUS ANTONINUS

Peace is not made in
documents, but in the
hearts of men.

HERBERT HOOVER

Glory to God in the highest,
and on earth peace, good
will toward men.

LUKE 2:14 (KJV)

Nothing on earth
Is more gentle and yielding
   than water,
Yet nothing is stronger.
When it confronts a wall
   of stone
Gentleness overcomes
   hardness;
The power of water prevails.

TAO 78

The first and fundamental
law of nature is to seek
peace and follow it.

THOMAS HOBBES

Peace: the soft and holy
shadow that virtue casts.

JOSH BILLINGS

We become the means of peace when we are willing to learn, to teach, to give, and especially to forgive.

FRANCES VAUGHAN
AND ROGER WALSH

Our most basic common link is that we all inhabit this small planet. We all breathe the same air. We all cherish our children's future. And we are all mortal.

JOHN FITZGERALD KENNEDY

When we do not find peace
within ourselves, it is vain to
seek for it elsewhere.

LA ROCHEFOUCAULD

Pray for your friends, but by all means pray for your enemies. And don't pray that they'll change; pray that *you* might change, from an accusatory mind to a loving one.

MARIANNE WILLIAMSON

Yesterday is but a dream, tomorrow is but a vision. But today well lived makes every yesterday a dream of happiness and every tomorrow a vision of hope. Look well, therefore, to this day.

SANSKRIT PROVERB

First the mind has to be quiet, control it, don't let it wander, because when you have a quiet mind life is extraordinary.

J. KRISHNAMURTI

If you want to know the
closest place to look for
grace, it is within yourself.
If you desire wisdom greater
than your own, you can find
it inside of you.

M. SCOTT PECK

Go outside, sit down on some grass or dirt, . . . take a deep breath, filling up with the gift of air. Soon, you will feel your connection to wholeness, and you will know peace.

BARBARA DEANGELIS

No ease there is higher than peace.

THE DHAMMAPADA 15.6

We can never gain any
peace of mind until we
secure our own soul.

MARGARET CHASE SMITH

Peace of mind has nothing
to do with the external
world; it has only to do with
our connection with God.

GERALD JAMPOLSKY

Inner peace and love are
the greatest of God's gifts.

TENTON SIOUX PROVERB

Have courage for the great sorrows of life and patience for the small ones; and when you have laboriously accomplished your daily task, go to sleep in peace. God is awake.

VICTOR HUGO

We limit ourselves by think-
ing that things can't be
done. Many think peace in
the world is impossible—
many think that inner peace
cannot be attained. It's the
one who doesn't know it
can't be done who does it!

PEACE PILGRIM

When peace is welcomed, it brings with it many gifts, among them healing, freedom, and love. Like peace, these gifts cannot be kept for ourselves alone but rather must be shared with others if we are to know them as our own.

FRANCES VAUGHAN
AND ROGER WALSH

Be good to those who are good
And to those who are not.
For goodness increases
   goodness.
Have faith in those who are
   faithful
And in those who are not.
For faith brings greater faith
And goodness and faith build
   peace.

TAO 49

Peaceful be earth, peaceful heaven, peaceful waters, peaceful trees. . . . I render peaceful whatever here is terrible, whatever here is cruel, whatever here is sinful. Let it become auspicious, let everything be beneficial to us.

HINDU PRAYER,
TENTH CENTURY B.C.

Her ways are ways of pleasantness, and all her paths are peace.

PROVERBS 3:17 (KJV)

Peace I leave with you, my peace I give unto you: not as the world giveth, give I unto you.

JOHN 14:27 (KJV)

For Mercy has a human
    heart,
Pity a human face,
And Love, the human form
    divine,
And Peace, the human
    dress.

WILLIAM BLAKE

Within the sphere of peace
there is no engine stronger
than love.

ANONYMOUS

Climb the mountains and
get their good tidings.
Nature's peace will flow into
you as the sunshine flows
into trees. The winds will
blow their own freshness
into you, and the storms
their energy, while cares will
drop away from you like the
leaves of Autumn.

JOHN MUIR

Over all the mountain tops
is peace.

JOHANN WOLFGANG VON GOETHE

If there is to be peace on earth and good will toward man we must finally believe in the ultimate morality of the universe and believe that all reality hinges on moral foundations.

DR. MARTIN LUTHER KING, JR.

Blessed are the peacemak-
ers: for they shall be called
the children of God.

A man is in a state of peace
when he renders good for
good, as far as it lies in him
to do, and wishes harm to
no one.

BERNARD OF CLAIRVAUX

The more fully and perfect-
ly the soul is able to com-
pose itself in inward peace
and tranquillity, the more
firmly and tenaciously it will
adhere to . . . raising up to
the supreme light by means
of contemplation.

RICHARD OF ST. VICTOR

Little things seem nothing,
but they give peace, like
those meadow flowers which
individually seem odorless
but all together perfume
the air.

GEORGES BERNANOS

That is peace: to be able to
rest serenely in the storm!

Dr. Billy Graham

To be able to see the world
in the light of love, which
can only come from within,
is to live without fear, in
unshakable peace.

DEEPAK CHOPRA

Lord, make me an instrument of Your peace. Where there is hatred let me sow love; where there is injury, pardon; where there is doubt, faith; where there is despair, hope; where there is darkness, light; and where there is sadness, joy.

ST. FRANCIS OF ASSISI